St Antholin's Lectureship

Charity Lecture 2014

"Strangely Warmed"
Whitefield, Toplady, Simeon and Wesley's Arminian Campaigns

Lee Gatiss

"Strangely Warmed": Whitefield, Toplady, Simeon and Wesley's Arminian Campaigns © Lee Gatiss 2014

ISBN 978-1-906327-28-6

Cover photo © ABDESIGN

Published by the Latimer Trust December 2014

The Latimer Trust (formerly Latimer House, Oxford) is a conservative Evangelical research organisation within the Church of England, whose main aim is to promote the history and theology of Anglicanism as understood by those in the Reformed tradition. Interested readers are welcome to consult its website for further details of its many activities.

The Latimer Trust
c/o Oak Hill College
London N14 4PS UK
Registered Charity: 1084337
Company Number: 4104465
Web: www.latimertrust.org
E-mail: administrator@latimertrust.org

Views expressed in works published by The Latimer Trust are those of the authors and do not necessarily represent the official position of The Latimer Trust.

CONTENTS

1. Introduction..1
2. George Whitefield's reply to Wesley 6
3. Wesley's continuing campaigns 11
4. The Zanchi Tract War 13
5. Putting the daggers away: Simeon and Wesley............18
6. Conclusion..24
St. Antholin's Lectureship Charity Lectures 27

1. Introduction

December 2014 sees the 300th birthday of the great Anglican Evangelical evangelist, George Whitefield (1714-1770).[1] Whitefield has been rightly celebrated as one of the primary causes, humanly-speaking, of the Evangelical revival of the eighteenth century. His most recent biographer lauds him as America's spiritual founding father.[2] His name has been kept alive by evangelical Baptists and evangelical Presbyterians, especially in North America.[3] Yet he has been strangely neglected in large measure by English Anglicans, despite being a thoroughgoing Church of England man.[4]

This relative neglect of Whitefield may not be surprising, however, when we consider that early on, the eighteenth-century evangelists were often barred from Anglican pulpits. One of those places seems to have been St. Helen's, Bishopsgate, which today has something of a reputation as a flagship evangelical church (and hosted some of the early revived St Antholin Lectures). More than once when I was on the staff there I was told the story of how graceless and dead St. Helen's must have been in those heady days of the revival. Why? Well, John Wesley came to preach at St Helen's one

---

[1] On behalf of the Trustees, I would like to thank Dr Mike Ovey and Dr Seulgi Byun of Oak Hill Theological College, London for hosting the 2014 St Antholin's Lecture at their Faculty and Postgraduate Seminar on 11th December, a few days before Whitefield's actual birthday.
[2] Thomas Kidd, *George Whitefield: America's Spiritual Founding Father* (Yale: Yale University Press, 2014).
[3] For example, the Banner of Truth published his journals and a (surprisingly) small selection of his sermons. And Whitefield's greatest biographer is the Canadian Baptist, Arnold Dallimore.
[4] See Lee Gatiss, "George Whitefield - the *Anglican* Evangelist" in *The Southern Baptist Journal of Theology* 18.2 (2014), pp.71-81.

Tuesday lunchtime in May 1738, and afterwards he wrote in his diary that someone said to him, "Sir you must preach here no more."[5]

Obviously the doctrines of grace and salvation were despised and misunderstood in eighteenth-century Bishopsgate! Yet I was always intrigued by this, so I did a bit of research. I read George Whitefield's journals and I found that he had preached at St. Helen's as well, one Sunday afternoon in August 1736, and had been received far more favourably. In one of his journal entries he says that as he ascended the stairs to the pulpit he felt they sneered at him on account of his youth but, "they soon grew serious and exceedingly attentive." It ended well, for Whitefield: "After I came down, [they] showed me great tokens of respect, blessed me as I passed along, and made great inquiry who I was."[6]

What was going on? Why, if Whitefield was received so well, was Wesley not also embraced at this clearly evangelical church?[7] What was I missing about the Evangelical Revival? The problem, I later

---

[5] Journal entry for Tuesday 9th May 1738 in T. Jackson (ed.), *The Works of John Wesley* (14 vols; Grand Rapids: Baker, 2007), vol.1: p.93. The Sunday before he had been told something similar by those at nearby St. Lawrence's and St. Katherine Cree, having been "enabled to speak strong words at both."

[6] G. Whitefield, *George Whitefield's Journals: A new edition containing fuller material than any hitherto published* (Edinburgh: Banner of Truth, 1960), p.77. He also narrates how dazed he was by the size of the church and the congregation at first, but was calmed by "considering in whose name I was about to speak."

[7] See my *The Tragedy of 1662*, (London: Latimer trust, 2007), pp.30, 39, 43-48 on Arthur Barham, the Presbyterian Vicar of St. Helen's, ejected in 1662. The sermons of one of his puritan successors, Dr. Thomas Horton (Rector from 1666), also demonstrate that predestination, penal substitution, particular atonement, the imputation of the active obedience of Christ, irresistible grace, the importance of promiscuous gospel preaching to all, and the necessity of the new birth were all previously proclaimed in the same City pulpit from which Wesley asserted his Arminianism in 1738. See e.g. T. Horton, *Forty-six Sermons upon the Whole Eighth Chapter of the Epistle of the Apostle Paul to the Romans* (London, 1674), pp.9-14, 50, 501-503. That Erasmus Middleton, a graduate of Kingswood School, one of the six students ejected from Oxford because of his Calvinistic Methodism in 1769, and Toplady's successor as editor of the Calvinist *Gospel Magazine*, was also a Lecturer at St. Helen's, also reveals something of where the church was theologically in the eighteenth century.

found, is that the controversy started by John Wesley in his strangely heated opposition to Reformed Anglican doctrine, has been systematically hushed up and played down by historians and hagiographers alike.[8] So much so, that opposition to Wesley is even now taken by some with little knowledge of Wesley's actual teaching to be straightforward opposition to the gospel itself.

I was less surprised, however, at the strong reactions against Mr. Wesley when I tracked down the printed version of his sermon on Romans 8:32, which is the text he preached on at St. Helen's in May 1738. It is a sermon he used on many occasions. From start to finish it is a sustained, emotive, combative, highly prejudiced and somewhat patronizing rant against Reformed doctrine, Calvinism. He went on and on about how believing in predestination was bad for your spiritual health and that it destroyed all zeal for good works, especially the good work of evangelism. No-one will evangelize if they believe in predestination, he asserted.

Predestination, Wesley pronounced, was "a doctrine full of blasphemy." He complained bitterly against "the horrible blasphemies contained in this horrible doctrine." To those who might disagree with his convictions he said, "You represent God as worse than the devil; more false, more cruel, more unjust... no scripture can prove predestination... I abhor the doctrine of predestination." He then went on to portray those who believe in the Reformed doctrine of predestination as worse than the baby-sacrificing worshippers of the false god Moloch. And this is not just a brief, off-the-cuff aside –

---

[8] See my survey of the histories by Bebbington, Gibson, Ryle, Balleine, and Noll in *The True Profession of the Gospel: Augustus Toplady and Reclaiming our Reformed Foundations* (London: Latimer Trust, 2010), pp.33-35.

this is the tenor of the whole sermon, and the reason it was published.⁹

Well, I have to say that doing a bit of historical research has certainly changed my mind about where St. Helen's stood in the eighteenth century. My sympathies are clearly with the discerning minister or churchwarden who sought to protect the church from hearing such divisive and melodramatic things again. If I'd been there, I think I too would have said, "Sir you must preach here no more."

Julia Wedgwood's 19th century biography of Wesley makes the rather insightful comment that Wesley's sermon against predestination has "in it something of that provoking glibness with which young or half-cultivated people settle in a few sentences questions that have exercised the deepest minds ever since the dawn of speculation... Indeed, it is evident on reading this sermon that, of all the deep works which had been written on the subject, Wesley had never read one."¹⁰

And yet he pronounced so forcefully on these weighty issues. This sermon was printed and reprinted many times in the following years, despite the howls of protest from Whitefield and others who pleaded with Wesley not to publish it at all.

Now, it has been suggested to me that Wesley just didn't understand grace when he preached like this in 1738. His heart had yet to be "strangely warmed" by the gospel when he had his so-called "Aldersgate experience", at St Botolph's, Aldersgate near St Paul's Cathedral in the City of London. It is true that the St Helen's sermon

---

9   See *The Works of John Wesley*, vol.7: pp.380-383. See the startling accusations in his hymn "Universal Redemption" about such people too: "Whoe'er admits; my soul disowns, The image of a torturing God, Well-pleased with human shrieks and groans, A fiend, a Molock gorged with blood! Good God! that any child of Thine, So horribly should think of Thee! Lo! all my hopes I here resign, If all may not find grace with me."
10 J. Wedgwood, *John Wesley and the Evangelical Reaction of the Eighteenth Century* (London: Macmillan, 1870), pp.226-227.

was on May 9th, and the reported warming of Wesley's heart was not to happen until May 24th. However, he disliked predestination, just like his mother, from very early on.[11] Iain Murray rightly notes that "Wesley's opposition to Calvinism stiffened rather than weakened."[12] His heart was always strangely warmed against it.

Wesley was, always would be, and always had been an Arminian. Arminians were fiercely opposed to things like unconditional predestination which they regarded as Calvinist nonsense. So Wesley printed this sermon and several other polemical works time and time again. Not just in 1738. But in 1739 and 1740 as well, when the revival was in full swing. He published about a dozen explicitly anti-Calvinist, anti-predestination works just in the few months after Whitefield's return to England after a mission to America. It was a deliberate ploy to mock, caricature, and oppose Reformed theology, and especially "the hellish doctrine" of predestination:

> O Horrible decree,
> Worthy of whence it came!
> Forgive their hellish blasphemy
> Who charge it on the Lamb.[13]

Wesley's line was that 'God told me to preach and print this'. He had cast lots and received very clear guidance, he said, to "preach and print" against predestination. The truth is though, it was all part of a rather sad and sordid power-play against Whitefield, who had left the rather imperious Wesley to look after the nascent evangelical movement while he went to preach in America. While Whitefield was out of the way, Wesley used his position to gather followers,

---

[11] See M. Wellings, "Susannah Wesley, 1669-1742," in A. Atherstone (ed.), *The Heart of Faith: Following Christ in the Church of England* (Cambridge: Lutterworth, 2008), pp.64-65.

[12] I. H. Murray, *Wesley and Men Who Followed* (Edinburgh: Banner of Truth, 2003), p.68.

[13] From Wesley's hymn, "The Horrible Decree" published in 1741. See J. R. Tyson, *Assist Me to Proclaim: The Life and Hymns of Charles Wesley* (Grand Rapids: Eerdmans, 2007), pp.99-116 on how the Wesleys' hymns opposed "the poison of Calvin".

pressurise booksellers to stock his Arminian tracts,[14] and form his own movement instead.

His distinctive rallying calls were his stance against predestination and his teaching on perfectionism. Arnold Dallimore's biography of Whitefield tells the full story in all its crude and shocking detail, of how Wesley tried to stamp his own mark and authority on the revival, and put himself at its head.[15] One of the things he did during this period was preach incessantly on the classic texts at issue between Calvinists and Arminians, such as 1 Timothy 2:3-6, John 1:29, and 1 John 2:2.[16] He was warmed to the fight.

2. George Whitefield's reply to Wesley

Whitefield was extremely reluctant to enter the lists against Wesley on this subject. Yet eventually, when Wesley had turned up the heat too far, he felt constrained to offer a reply in a public letter to Wesley.[17] It was clear, courteous, and effective. What's more it was very restrained and mildly put in comparison with Wesley's bitter invective, especially when that is read in the context of Wesley's shenanigans in attempting to hijack and take over Whitefield's movement while he was abroad. One of the things he criticises Wesley for is ignoring the actual text he was meant to be preaching on:

> Had any one a mind to prove the doctrine of *election,* as well as of *final perseverance,* he could hardly wish for a text more fit for his

---

[14] See Wesley's letter to James Hutton in A. Dallimore, *George Whitefield: The Life and Times of the Great Evangelist of the 18th Century Revival* (2 vols.; Edinburgh: Banner of Truth, 1970), vol.1: p.314.
[15] See Dallimore, *George Whitefield,* vol.1: pp.306-319 and vol.2: pp.18-41.
[16] See *The Works of John Wesley,* vol.1: pp.188-193 (April -May 1739).
[17] Dallimore, *George Whitefield* vol.2: pp.551-569 and *George Whitefield's Journals,* pp.563-588. See also several earlier private letters in Dallimore, *George Whitefield,* vol.1: pp.571-581.

purpose, than that which you have chosen to disprove it. One that does not know you would suspect you yourself was [sic] sensible of this: for after the first paragraph, I scarce know whether you have mentioned it so much as once, through your whole sermon.[18]

Whitefield refers to several books which he thinks helpful and unanswerable on the points in question. Clearly he *had* read some deep works written on the subject, and encourages Wesley more than once to go and do likewise. Whitefield even sent Wesley copies of books which he thought he might find helpful in answering his objections. Whitefield was standing on the shoulders of giants in the Puritan and Reformed tradition.

Wesley, who obviously identified Whitefield with the wider Reformed tradition, wrote that no Baptist or Presbyterian writer he had read knew anything of the liberties of Christ.[19] Whitefield counters this by arguing that Wesley's sermon associated him with a different tradition: Your idea of "universal redemption is a notion sadly adapted to keep the soul in its lethargic sleepy condition, and therefore so many natural men admire and applaud it," he wrote, "Infidels of all kinds are on your side of the question. Deists, Arians, Socinians, arraign God's sovereignty, and stand up for universal redemption." He then cites Article 17 to show that "our godly reformers did not think election destroyed holiness" and questions Wesley's loyalty to the Reformed Church of England saying, "I cannot but blame you for censuring the clergy of our church for not keeping to their articles, when you yourself by your principles, positively deny the 9th, 10th, and 17th."[20]

Whitefield's response places him very firmly in what we can call the Reformed tradition of the Church of England. So he says, for instance:

---

[18] Dallimore, *George Whitefield* vol.2: p.555; emphasis original.
[19] His father had once been imprisoned for speaking so furiously against the Dissenters, and John Wesley obviously shared his opinion of nonconformists.
[20] Dallimore, *George Whitefield* vol.2: pp.559-569.

"But, blessed be God, our Lord knew for whom he died. There was an eternal compact between the Father and the Son. A certain number was then given him, as the purchase and reward of his obedience and death. For these he prayed, John xvii, and not for the world. For these, and these only, he is now interceding, and with their salvation he will be fully satisfied."[21]

You can see why the hymn writer Toplady says that Whitefield was not only a great evangelist but also "a most excellent systematic divine."[22] This is careful, covenantal, Calvinist divinity, preached with passion and fervour.

In the rest of his reply, Whitefield shows several times why he thinks such doctrines are a very good thing in terms of *encouraging* a godly life and spurring us on to evangelism – rather than being a bad thing as Wesley had alleged. Predestination, rather than something to be abhorred, was Whitefield's daily comfort and support, he said. This is warm piety allied to solid theology, all served up in a firm but friendly tone.

In one of his sermons Whitefield talks about those who dislike this sort of Reformed theology.

"They that are not led to see this, I wish them better heads; though, I believe, numbers that are against it have got better hearts: the Lord help us to bear with one another where there is an honest heart."[23]

But Wesley hated all this. Wesley's great grandfather was a well-known Puritan, John White. And Wesley's grandfather, Samuel Annesley, was a Puritan, nonconformist minister. He had a little meeting room in St. Helen's Place, right next door to St Helen's, Bishopsgate. But Wesley's parents quickly abandoned their

---

[21] Dallimore, *George Whitefield* vol.2: p.568.
[22] A. M. Toplady, *The Complete Works of Augustus Toplady* (Harrisburg, Virginia: Sprinkle Publications, 1987), p.494.
[23] Lee Gatiss (ed.), *The Sermons of George Whitefield* (2 vols; Watford: Church Society, 2010), vol.2: p.452.

evangelical and puritan roots. His father was a Church of England clergyman, and John Wesley called himself a High Churchman born of High Church parents.[24] He was brought up to despise the Reformed faith and his puritan heritage.

Now, let's be clear on all this. Wesley may well have believed in all the objective facts of salvation such as substitutionary atonement and the bodily resurrection of Christ. But he wasn't just mistaken about 'small' things like predestination; he was also confused about Christian perfection, which he taught as being attainable in this life, and he even wobbled on the doctrine of justification by faith alone.

So if we go forward to Wesley's Methodist Conference in 1770, we find Wesley had been losing patience with the Evangelical Calvinists. He chose this moment, the year when George Whitefield died, to return to the Arminian distinctives, but particularly to justification and its relationship to holiness with which he had been wrestling. The Minutes of the Conference were, Jim Packer says, "so drafted as to appear to teach, Roman-style, that a man's works are the ground of his acceptance with God." For example, as well as rebuking the Methodists for leaning "too much towards Calvinism," (a poisonous plague which was worse than all the devices of Satan) Wesley told them this:

> "every believer, till he comes to glory, works *for*, as well as *from*, life... We have received it as a maxim that 'a man is to do nothing in order to justification.' Nothing can be more false... Is not this salvation by works? Not by the *merit* of works, but by works as a *condition*... we are every hour and every moment pleasing or displeasing to God, 'according to our works'."[25]

---

[24] John Telford (ed.), *The Letters of John Wesley* (8 vols; London, Epworth Press, 1931) vol.5: p.156.

[25] J. I. Packer, "Arminianisms," in *Honouring the People of God* (vol. 4 of *Collected Shorter Works of J. I. Packer*; Carlisle: Paternoster, 1999), p.301. For the text of the Minutes see e.g. F. Cook, *Selina Countess of Huntingdon: Her Pivotal Role in the 18th Century Evangelical Awakening* (Edinburgh: Banner of Truth, 2001), pp.278-279.

Read that again, slowly: we do good works *for* eternal life, not just spurred on by a new birth; it is false to say that we contribute nothing to our justification (i.e. it is not by faith alone); good works are a condition of our salvation.

This sort of assertion is rightly shocking to those taught to value our Reformation heritage. So, writes Iain Murray,

> "If Wesley's theology was confused, why, some might ask, should we value his memory today? The answer is that it is not in his theology that his real legacy lies. Christian leaders are raised up for different purposes. The eighteenth century evangelicals were primarily men of action, and in that role, John Wesley did and said much which was to the lasting benefit of many thousands."[26]

That may be true, in a way. But we may also want to go on and ask whether celebrity men of action can really be so easily excused a little dodgy theology on basic issues of salvation.

George Whitefield on the other hand, though he was rather prone to some dramatic excesses in his early years, was to my mind a much more admirable figure.[27] His Reformed theology gave his message and preaching a depth and stability that Wesley lacked. While Wesley's influence would spread far and wide across the globe, much of Whitefield's lasting legacy remained within the Church of England, and the evangelical movement. Most of the conforming evangelicals and those in the Countess of Huntingdon's Connexion were Reformed in theology like Whitefield.

---

[26] Murray, *Wesley and Men Who Followed*, p.79.
[27] He himself admits that he spoke in a style "too apostolical" in his early days, and as difficult as it might have been for a celebrity preacher, he publicly repented of it. See *The Works of the Reverend George Whitefield*: vol.2 (1771): p.144. See also *George Whitefield's Journals*, p.462 note 1 on retractions from his journals concerning his overly hasty, 'rash and uncharitable,' assessment of some American theologians. Some say Whitefield was merely an entertainer or dramatist, with little interest in theology, e.g. H. S. Stout, *The Divine Dramatist: George Whitefield and the Rise of Modern Evangelicalism* (Grand Rapids: Eerdmans, 1991). But this is palpable nonsense!

3. Wesley's continuing campaigns

Now, it would be bad enough if Wesley and Whitefield fell out — the two great names in the Evangelical Revival — and at the height of all the awakening activity. But what if Wesley continued to press his case for Arminianism even further? What else would happen? Let's look further at Wesley's controversial campaigns, to put his spat with Whitefield into some kind of context. They are sometimes known as 'the Calvinist controversies'. But that label was obviously invented to make Calvinism look as if *it* was the trouble-maker. Others at the time did not see it that way: they saw that the problem was Wesley's Arminianism and his campaigns to promote it. It was he who, in Whitefield's words, threw in the bone of contention.

The first Arminian controversy was that cold war between Wesley and Whitefield in the 1740s. In the 1750s, James Hervey for the Reformed was attacked by John Fletcher and others for the Arminians.[28] This was round two. Round three, however, would see Wesley go up against the most able of all those on the Calvinist side of the debate: Augustus Montague Toplady. He is most famous as a hymn writer. He wrote *A Debtor to Mercy Alone* and the startling and oft-quoted lines, "Nothing in my hand I bring, simply to thy cross I cling." But he was also a preacher, a historian, and a controversialist of great talent.

Toplady linked Arminian theology to Pelagius, the arch-heretic who had opposed Augustine in the fourth century. Some might find this offensive perhaps, but Wesley was in fact happy to identify with Pelagius, one of the righteous remnant in church history, a true Christian, a holy man, who had been unfairly stigmatized by the nasty abusive Augustine (who wasn't worth listening to). All Pelagius was trying to say, averred Wesley, was that a Christian can go on to

---

[28] See J. Hervey, *Aspasio Vindicated in Eleven Letters from Mr. Hervey to the Rev. John Wesley* (London, J & F Rivington, 1764) for an example of the literature from this second phase of the Arminian controversies.

perfection and fulfil the law of Christ.[29] Toplady also linked Arminianism to Rome. Indeed, he said, "Arminianism is the forerunner which prepares the way for Rome, and, if not discarded in time, will one day open the door to it."[30]

J. C. Ryle seems to consider Toplady's identification of Arminians with Pelagians and Papists a scandalous outrage.[31] In fact, Ryle has done more than anyone to destroy Toplady's reputation because of this, in his popular book on the Christian leaders of the eighteenth century. Yet these were, of course, not unusual connections to make in the sixteenth, seventeenth, or eighteenth centuries. Whitefield (whom Ryle loves), John Gill, and many others also drew attention to the theological links, and it had been standard practice in the Puritan debates against Laudianism and the Remonstrants.[32]

It was also not unusual when elsewhere Toplady linked the rise of immorality in the country with the rise of Arminianism in the Church, especially under the Merry Monarch, Charles II.[33] Was that outrageous? Well, if it was, we should also point out that several leading Arminian Methodists including Wesley accused Calvinists of all manner of evils, alleging they were unchristian, heretical, Islamic, fatalistic, cold and emotionless sloths whose principles proved they

---

[29] *The Works of John Wesley*, vol.6: pp.328-329.
[30] Toplady, *Complete Works*, pp.661-662.
[31] J. C. Ryle, *Christian Leaders of the Eighteenth Century* (Edinburgh: Banner of Truth, 1978 [1885]), p.380.
[32] Books were published in the 17th century with names like *A parallel: of new-old Pelgiarminian error and Pelagius redivivus*: or *Pelagius raked out of the ashes by Arminius and his schollers* (these both by Daniel Featley in 1626). John Owen's first publication in 1642 was called *A Display of Arminianism: Being a Discovery of the Old Pelagian Idol, Free Will, with the New Goddess Contingency, Advancing Themselves into the Throne of the God of Heaven, to the Prejudice of his Grace.*
[33] Toplady, *Complete Works*, p.278. "Let the clergy learn to despise the sinful pleasures, maxims, pursuits, and doctrines of the world; and the world will, from that moment, cease to despise the clergy," Toplady wrote to the Bench of Bishops. "Your lordships observe with pain the glaring and almost universal decay of moral virtue. — this has been a growing calamity, ever since the restoration of the Stuart line in the person of Charles II. With that prince, Arminianism returned as a flood; and licentiousness of manners was co-extensive with it."

must be uninterested in evangelism and such like. So accusing *them* of a tendency to Pelagianism (an identification Wesley appeared happily to accept) hardly seems comparable on the insult scale.

4. The Zanchi Tract War

Toplady and Wesley came to blows in print between 1769 and 1772, in what I call the Zanchi Tract War.

In November 1769, Toplady published a translation of a work on predestination by Jerome Zanchius (1516-1590) which he entitled *The Doctrine of Absolute Predestination Stated and Asserted*. This had been influential in his own spiritual development while he was a student and he had originally translated it in 1760, when he was 19. After some prompting from his Baptist friend John Gill and others he overcame his diffidence and decided the time was now right to publish this translation.

Zanchi's book leans heavily on Luther's reply to Erasmus on the bondage of the will, as well as on Augustine, and covers election, reprobation, particular redemption, and various objections to those doctrines, concluding with a section promoting promiscuous gospel preaching to all and public teaching on predestination for the saints. The ultimate reason for focusing on this doctrine, he said, was that "scarce any other distinguishing doctrine of the gospel can be preached in its purity and consistency without this of predestination."[34]

A few months later, John Wesley wrote to his Methodist colleague Walter Sellon. He had already asked Sellon to write something against John Owen's work on limited atonement or particular redemption, disliking that doctrine intensely. He tasked Sellon with writing against Toplady as well, "in order to stop the mouth of that

---

[34] Toplady, *Complete Works*, p.704.

vain boaster." Evidently Wesley felt threatened by the arrival of the much younger Toplady on the scene.[35]

It was Wesley himself, however, who made the most public response to the translation of Zanchi. He put out an abridgement of Toplady's work with the same title and published under Toplady's own name (but for his own profit).[36] Three observations ought to be made on this abridgement. First, it does capture something of the general flow of Zanchius' argument and retain a few of the choicest quotations; as revision notes for an exam on Zanchius' philosophy this material might have some use.

Second, however, Wesley removes entirely the biblical aspect of Zanchi's presentation. For example, in Toplady's translation there are around 350 quotations and citations from Scripture, around which the whole argument is built. In Wesley's abridgement there is just one biblical allusion ("Esau have I hated") and that without giving the reference. This leaves an entirely different taste in the mouth and castrates the persuasive potential of the work for Christian readers.

Finally, and most alarmingly, Wesley himself added a whole paragraph to the book, which was all his own work and seemed calculated to paint both predestination and Augustus Toplady in as bad a light as possible.

> "The sum of all is this: One in twenty (suppose) of mankind are elected; nineteen in twenty are reprobated. The elect shall be saved, do what they will: The reprobate shall be damned, do what they can. Reader, believe this, or be damned. Witness my hand, A_T_."[37]

---

[35] *The Works of John Wesley*, vol.13: pp.44-45. In *The Letters of John Wesley*: vol.5: p.167 this letter also contains Wesley's description of Toplady as a "lively coxcomb" (a conceited, showy person).

[36] "The Doctrine of Absolute Predestination Stated and Asserted by the Reverend Mr. A_T_," in *The Works of John Wesley*, vol.14: pp.190-198.

[37] "The Doctrine of Absolute Predestination Stated and Asserted by the Reverend Mr. A_T_," in *The Works of John Wesley*, vol.14: p.191.

Naturally, Toplady felt somewhat aggrieved by this gross misrepresentation. He replied to Wesley, pointing out that "In almost any other case, a similar forgery would transmit the criminal to Virginia or Maryland, if not to Tyburn."[38] There were harsh laws at the time against forgery, which did indeed lead to the execution at Tyburn of one of Mr. Wesley's acquaintances in 1777. But Toplady thought it better to refute Wesley's falsehoods than take him to court for his plagiaristic libel.

As far as this infamous final paragraph was concerned, for example, the numbers were wrong (and presumptuous!) and certainly not Toplady's. In Toplady's opinion, "The kingdom of glory will both be more largely and more variously peopled than bigots of all denominations are either able to think, or willing to allow."[39] Wesley's summary of what he had written was also scurrilous, with entirely false implications. The elect are not saved "do what they will" but "chosen as much to holiness as to heaven."[40]

Equally importantly, Toplady neither claimed nor thought that Arminians were all going to hell.[41] He never said one had to be a Calvinist to be saved. That, of course, would have been a strange thing for him to assert, given that he was an Arminian himself for several years after his conversion and does not subsequently re-date his conversion to the year he became a Calvinist. He thought many Arminians were "pious, moderate, respectable men," adding, "Of these I myself know more than a few: and have the happiness to

---

[38] Toplady, *Complete Works*, p.721. "If such an opponent can be deemed an honest man," he continues, "where shall we find a knave?" Being sent to the American plantations for hard labour was a severe punishment; Tyburn was a central London venue for hangings.
[39] Toplady, *Complete Works*, p.726.
[40] Toplady, *Complete Works*, p.735.
[41] J. C. Ryle, *Christian Leaders*, p.380 seems uncritically to buy Wesley's misrepresentation when he claims that Toplady "appears to think it impossible that an Arminian can be saved." Ironically, given Ryle's rather superior censure of Toplady, this completely overlooks all Toplady's positive statements to the contrary (just as he overlooks all Wesley's violently negative language about Calvinists).

enjoy as much of their esteem, as they deservedly possess of mine." He can even be very positive about some other prominent Arminians, calling them eminent and worthy, "great ornaments to our church," and not to be mentioned without honour, even while he disagrees fervently with their Arminianism.[42]

Wesley replied to Toplady's reply, and so on. It was a tract war. One commentator says that "Toplady treated Wesley with the manners and decorum of a gentleman and the analytical objectivity of a scientist."[43] He may have been slightly warmer than that. But what was he up against? At one point, Wesley compares the Calvinist God to a man who has his enemy's nine year old daughter raped so he can then strangle her to death because she has been 'deflowered'.[44] Toplady rightly thought this impious (to say the least), and some evangelicals refused to allow Wesley to preach in their churches because of this. Toplady complained against "a man who is so liberally lamentable in his outcries against the doctrine of predestination, and carries to such horrid length his invectives against the purposes and providence of God."[45]

It is no surprise that some Evangelicals refused to allow Wesley to use their churches. Toplady's attempts at persuasion won him no friends amongst the Arminians, but he continued to pray for them and hope for them. He wrote to a friend in 1773 that "The envy, malice, and fury of Wesley's party are inconceivable. But, violently as they hate me, I dare not, I cannot, hate them in return. I have not so learned Christ. – They have my prayers and my best wishes for their

---

[42] See Toplady, *Complete Works*, pp.275, 389, 614-615, 730, 732.
[43] G. M. Ella, *Augustus Montague Toplady: A Debtor to Mercy Alone* (Eggleston, Durham: Go Publications, 2000), p.34.
[44] *The Works of John Wesley*, vol.10: p.373. This may be an allusion to the note in Suetonius's life of the Roman emperor, Tiberius (*Suet. Tib.* 61.5): *immaturae puellae, quia more tradito nefas esset uirgines strangulari, uitiatae prius a carnifice, dein strangulatae* ("Since, according to an ancient tradition, it was sinful to strangle virgins, the young girls were first deflowered by the executioner, before being strangled").
[45] Toplady, *Complete Works*, pp.761, 756.

present and eternal salvation. But their errors have my opposition also."[46]

Toplady's reputation has been unfairly maligned in my opinion because the extravagant Arminian eccentricities of the great and famous John Wesley have been hushed up or too easily excused – by Wesley, his followers, by Ryle, and others. It certainly does seem out of place for a man ordained nearly 50 years to behave the way Wesley did towards a fellow-Evangelical less than half his age. As Packer rightly says, Wesley's misrepresentations of Calvinism "argue a degree of prejudice and closed-mindedness which is almost pathological."[47] His heart was hot with hatred for Calvinism.

Toplady wrote to a friend after all this, "I believe Wesley to be the most rancorous hater of the gospel-system that ever appeared in this island. I except not Pelagius himself."[48] But as a young man in his twenties he had held back from publishing his translation of Zanchi for nine long years, fearful of offending Wesley and those on his side.[49] If anything, Toplady seems for many years to have been guilty of an unwarranted deference to the older man's celebrity and intimidating influence.

If in later years this may have threatened to become an unhealthy fixation on demonstrating Wesley's perfidious errors, we can also see

---

[46] Toplady, *Complete Works*, p.840. See also pp.46, 839.
[47] Packer, "Arminianisms," in *Honouring the People of God*, p.300.
[48] Toplady, *Complete Works*, p.847.
[49] He had fulfilled what Horace recommended (Horace, *De Arte Poetica*, 385-390): "*siquid tamen olim scripseris, in Meti descendat iudicis auris et patris et nostras nonumque prematur in annum membranis intus positis: delere licebit, quod non edideris, nescit vox missa reverti.*" Basically, if you write anything, let a few other trusted friends read it, and sit on it for nine years. You can always change or delete things which you haven't published yet, but you can't take it back once it's "out there." This is also recommended at the start of Quintillian, *Institutio Oratoria*, because it enables authors to let the excitement of writing cool down and gives time for dispassionate revision. Toplady says he delayed, however, not in order to come back to the work in a calmer mood, but because he was "not sufficiently delivered from the fear of man". There is much here for modern bloggers and writers to ponder!

with crystal clarity that what also motivated Toplady was defending the gospel of God's mercy and grace. It was even his duty, he thought, to pray for Wesley, writing, "O, that He, in whose hand the hearts of all men are, may make even this opposer of grace a monument of almighty power to save! God is witness how earnestly I wish it may consist with the divine will to touch the heart and open the eyes of that unhappy man."[50]

5. Putting the daggers away: Simeon and Wesley

I originally gave this lecture the somewhat more sensationalist title, "Celebrity preachers in Calvinist cover-ups." The extent of Wesley's Arminianism and bad behaviour has for too long been covered up. We have explored some reasons why already, but much of the blame for downplaying things here might fairly be laid at the door of another evangelical Anglican hero, Charles Simeon.

In November 1787, nearly a decade after Toplady died, a young Charles Simeon, destined to be the leader of the Evangelicals into the next century, met with the aging John Wesley. The conversation (though it is not recounted in Wesley's journal) has often been cited as evidence that Calvinists and Arminians are in essence agreed on fundamentals:

Simeon: Sir, I understand that you are called an Arminian; and I have been sometimes called a Calvinist; and therefore I suppose we are to draw daggers. But before I consent to begin the combat, with your permission I will ask you a few questions, not from impertinent curiosity, but for real instruction. Pray, Sir, do you feel yourself a depraved creature, so depraved, that you would never have thought of turning unto God, if God had not first put it into your heart?

---

[50] Quoted in A. Brown-Lawson, *John Wesley and the Anglican Evangelicals of the Eighteenth Century: A Study in Cooperation and Separation with Special Reference to the Calvinistic Controversies* (Durham: Pentland Press, 1994), p.328.

Wesley: Yes, I do indeed.

Simeon: And do you utterly despair of recommending yourself to God by any thing you can do; and look for salvation solely through the blood and righteousness of Christ?

Wesley: Yes, solely through Christ.

Simeon: But, Sir, supposing you were first saved by Christ, are you not somehow or other to save yourself afterwards by your own works?

Wesley: No, I must be saved by Christ from first to last.

Simeon: Allowing then that you were first turned by the grace of God, are you not in some way or other to keep yourself by your own power?

Wesley: No.

Simeon: What then, are you to be upheld every hour and every moment by God, as much as an infant in its mother's arms?

Wesley: Yes; altogether.

Simeon: And is all your hope in the grace and mercy of God to preserve you unto his heavenly kingdom?

Wesley: Yes; I have no hope, but in him.

Simeon: Then, Sir, with your leave, I will put up my dagger again; for this is all my Calvinism; this is my election, my justification by faith, my final perseverance: it is, in substance, all that I hold, and as I hold it: and therefore, if you please, instead of searching out terms and phrases to be a ground of contention between us, we will cordially unite in those things wherein we agree.[51]

---

[51] The conversation is recounted in C. Simeon, *Helps to Composition, or Six Hundred Skeletons of Sermons* (1st American ed.; 5 vols.; Philadelphia, William W. Woodward, 1810), vol.1: p.xviii note o.

We ought to notice that Simeon begins (if this account is accurate and does actually relate to Simeon himself)[52] not by claiming to *be* a Calvinist but by saying he has "sometimes" been called one. Normally, he did not want to identify either with Calvinists or Arminians, claiming to be "no friend to systematizers in Theology..." He had "no doubt that there is a system in the Holy Scriptures; (for truth cannot be inconsistent with itself)," but he was "persuaded that neither Calvinists nor Arminians are in exclusive possession of that system."[53]

Wesley, on the other hand, who died about 20 years before Simeon published this conversation, identified Simeon, on both occasions when the two met, as very much like his own designated successor as leader of the Arminians, J. Fletcher of Madeley. Simeon and Fletcher are "two kindred souls," he says in 1784. Simeon "breathes the very spirit of Mr. Fletcher," he repeated in his journal in 1787.[54] That is not to say that Simeon was an Arminian, of course, only that his Calvinism was either unseen or sufficiently confused as to not attract the attention of the man who had been Calvinism's self-proclaimed nemesis for fifty years and had made such harsh pronouncements against it.

---

[52] The dialogue is prefaced, "A circumstance within the Author's knowledge reflects so much light upon this subject, that he trusts he shall be pardoned for relating it. A young minister, about three or four years after he was ordained, had an opportunity of conversing familiarly with the great and venerable leader of the Arminians in this kingdom; and, wishing to improve the occasion to the uttermost, he addressed him nearly in the following words..." It seems likely that it does refer to Simeon himself, but a small doubt remains due to the third person references.

[53] C. Simeon *Horae Homileticae or Discourses (in the Form of Skeletons) upon the Whole Scriptures* (17 vols.; London, Printed by Richard Watts, and sold by Cadell and Davies. 1819), vol.1: pp.4-5.

[54] *The Works of John Wesley*, vol.4: pp.294, 403. Since Simeon was ordained deacon in 1782 and priest in 1783 the conversation (if between Simeon and Wesley) took place between 1785-1787 (3-4 years after he was ordained, as he says), and hence the November 1787 meeting is the most likely occasion contra e.g. H. Moule, *Charles Simeon: Pastor of a Generation* (Fearn, Ross-shire: Christian Focus, 1997 [1892]), p.83 who dates it to 1784.

Perhaps Simeon was somewhat naïve in his youthful enthusiasm to sidestep decades of serious discussion and be considered (like a consummate ecclesiastical politician) sympathetic to both sides. Yet the debate was not, as many may wish it to be, one merely of timing and where to place the emphasis – as if Calvinists like Whitefield held to divine sovereignty but did not appeal for humans decisions, or that they simply ignored parts of Scripture that did not at first blush seem to fit their preconceived system, or that they were abstract theologisers who needed Arminians to teach them how to speak to real people. That caricature certainly does not fit George Whitefield, the greatest evangelist of the eighteenth century.

To say Arminian doctrines of free will could be used alongside Calvinist teaching concerning divine providence and grace as if they were not necessarily contradictory perhaps sounded irenic. Yet what are we to make of Simeon's comment that, "It is supposed by many, that the doctrines of grace are incompatible with the doctrine of man's free-will; and that therefore the one or the other must be false. But why so?" — or his assertion that, "it is possible, that the truth, may lie, not exclusively in either, nor yet in a confused mixture of both, but in the proper and seasonable application of them both."[55] It seems likely that Simeon's misunderstanding that the two systems could be pastorally blended to obtain a supposedly better, more biblical, balance played straight into synergistic Arminian hands, and I suspect the more experienced Wesley was well aware of this. Toplady would have said something like, "evangelical truth knows nothing of this harlequin assemblage."[56]

Second, it ought to be pointed out that Simeon, narrating events two decades previously, does most of the talking in this famous exchange, putting words into the older man's mouth. Hence we learn more here about Simeon than we do about Wesley. Very skilfully, he skirts round some of the actual areas of contention to present *himself* in a very positive light. For example, he asks whether Wesley "feels

---

[55] Simeon, *Helps to Composition*, pp.xvi, xxi.
[56] Toplady, *Complete Works*, p.722.

himself depraved" not whether he *is* or *was* totally depraved and unable to respond to God before his conversion which, because of his doctrine of prevenient grace or 'universal enablement,' he would not have been able to answer in the affirmative like a Calvinist.[57] As Charles Wesley's hymn appended to his brother's *Free Grace* sermon puts it:

> A power to choose, a will to obey,
> Freely His grace restores;
> We all may find the living way.
> And call the Saviour ours.[58]

As he re-sheaths his dagger Simeon declares, "this is all my Calvinism; this is my election." We should note, however, that he has at no point actually addressed the doctrine of election in the conversation! Presumably this is because he knew full well that Wesley believed in predestination on the basis of foreseen faith and perseverance, and not on the basis of God's gratuitous unmerited choice alone. As Charles Wesley would have us sing:

> Whom his eternal mind *foreknew*,
> That they the power would use,
> Ascribe to God the glory due,
> And not his grace refuse;
>
> Them, only them, his will decreed,
> Them did he *choose* alone,
> *Ordain'd* in Jesus' steps to tread,
> And be like his Son.

This is *conditional election based on foreseen faith* and the use of resistible grace by an unbound will. This was no small point, but goes

---

[57] See e.g. The Works of John Wesley, vol.6: pp.509, 512; 7:189; 10:229-230, 392.
[58] Also found in volume 1 of Wesley's *Arminian Magazine* (1778). Later, it says: "Lord, if indeed, without a bound, Infinite Love Thou art, The HORRIBLE DECREE confound, Enlarge Thy people's heart! Ah! who is as Thy servants blind, So to misjudge their God! Scatter the darkness of their mind, And shed Thy love abroad."

to the very heart of the predestination debate. In his noble and heroic crusade for some kind of unity, however, Simeon evidently feels it is merely "searching out terms and phrases to be a ground of contention." Admittedly, by the late eighteenth century some may have gone too far into an unhealthy hyper-Calvinism or into arguing about words in an unwholesome way. Yet there was real gospel-minded concern at the heart of people's concerns about Wesley, which is not apparent from the way Simeon deals with him here.

Third, it is hardly right to acquit Wesley (and Arminianism) of synergistic views of salvation simply on the basis of his own protestations and denials. Which Christian theologian ever admitted openly to teaching salvation by works? Yet that is not to say every Christian theologian avoids that trap or tendency as a clear implication of their system or in the minds of their less educated followers. Calvinists and Arminians alike need to guard themselves from inconsistency with their own profession and the dangers on either side of them.

Nevertheless, Simeon's view of Wesley and of Arminianism has become the dominant note in much of today's Evangelicalism. Differences between Calvinists and Arminians are too often evaded and fudged for the sake of unity and peace so that someone who dredges them up is considered factious and unnecessarily combative — "a cynic, a bear, a Toplady," as Wesley put it in his usual sour way.[59] It is remarkable how often individuals have covered a drift towards different forms of liberalism "with professions of indifference to theological aridities," as one writer so strikingly puts it.[60] Yet questioning someone's teaching on predestination, justification, and sanctification is hardly equivalent to arguing about how many angels can dance on the head of a pin.

---

[59] *The Works of John Wesley*, vol.10: p.414. He thought becoming a Calvinist made one "spiteful, morose, and touchy." This may be true of some people, of course; and true also of fractious men and women of all parties.
[60] A. Cromartie, 'Hale, Sir Mathew (1609–1676),' *Oxford Dictionary of National Biography* (Oxford: Oxford University Press, 2004).

6. Conclusion

Wesley raised the temperature of debate amongst evangelicals in the eighteenth century. For one supposedly devoted to evangelical unity and peace, his heart and pen were strangely warmed against Calvinists and Calvinism. His behaviour and tone have too often been excused or covered up, and many have been blinded by his celebrity and reputation, and wanted to keep him and his followers onside. That has sometimes led to something of a whitewash.

"Those who are for peace, will leave these things alone," Wesley once said. Many feel the same way about the Arminian controversies which he stirred up — it is better not to get embroiled in such things. When he said those words, however, Wesley was not trying to calm a doctrinal debate (which he continued to fuel) but deflect attention away from his scurrilous slandering of Toplady![61] Party loyalty may sometimes be laudable, and there is a time and a place; but the idea that for the sake of "evangelical unity" we must never question the behaviour of the big chiefs, however lamentable, is surely anathema to truth-loving Christians. Those that are for truth must sometimes touch the sore spot.

In my view, it is imperative that both Whitefield and Toplady are heard again in proper context by both Evangelicals and Anglicans. It is vital, as Paul Helm rightly notes, to see clearly that the Evangelical participants in the eighteenth century controversy, "certainly did not

---

[61] Wesley spread slanderous rumours that Toplady, on his death-bed aged only 38, had renounced his faith and wanted to repent of all he had said in opposition to Wesley. Toplady dragged himself out of bed to preach again, so as to refute this calumny. Once he was dead, Wesley spread further (false) rumours that he had died in black despair uttering blasphemies, and even wrote to Toplady's friends commiserating with them that their friend had died "a dud squib." He was pursued for an apology for all this by Sir Richard Hill and others (who had actually been with Toplady when he died), but all he would say in response was "Those that are for peace will let these things alone." For the whole sordid tale and Wesley's attempted cover-up, see Ella, *Augustus Montague Toplady*, pp.331-340.

think that what united them was greater than what divided them. The occurrence of the Calvinist-Arminian division was very serious, fairly permanent, and sad."[62] Many would not have considered themselves Evangelical first and Reformed second if that meant unity with the domineering Wesley was the touchstone issue. George Whitefield may acknowledge some common ground with Wesley, but he resisted the idea that the issues at stake between them on predestination, the atonement, perfectionism, original sin, and justification were of only secondary importance, to be placed on one side for the sake of a common witness. He told Wesley in 1741 that they were preaching two different gospels.[63]

Fred Sanders, a well-known and much respected Arminian Wesleyan, recently attacked Toplady in a blog post. Toplady wrote the hymn *Rock of Ages*, he said, "out of spite", and was "a bitter and narrow-minded young man who couldn't keep his personal hatred from over-flowing into his prayers and songs." Well, Toplady did indulge in some florid rhetoric at times, for which he cannot be entirely praised. Sometimes he didn't wrestle enough with 2 Timothy 2:22-26. But I think my friend Professor Sanders is perhaps guilty of selective historical judgment. Again, Toplady is excoriated (and not always fairly) while the great and famous John Wesley is almost automatically exonerated from his perfidious crimes! Dr Sanders does, however, have these very helpful words of application:

> "When publicly disagreeing with other believers, try to keep some sense of perspective. If a Wesleyan is the worst thing you can imagine, you have a weak imagination. Wesley's influence is not what's driving the godless spirit of the age. The same moral applies, of course, to Arminians, too: If you think the main problem with the world today is Calvinism, you should get

---

[62] P. Helm, "Calvin, A.M. Toplady and the Bebbington Thesis," in M. A. G. Haykin and K. J. Stewart (eds.), *The Emergence of Evangelicalism: Exploring Historical Continuities* (Nottingham: Apollos, 2008), p.215.
[63] *The Works of John Wesley*, vol.1: p.305.

out more."[64]

That being said, for Whitefield and his friends, the confessionally Anglican and evangelical testimony to God's saving grace in the gospel must remain unadulterated. Unconditional election and justification *sola fide* are too important to push conveniently to one side. A time may come when even friends or allies must be taken to task for "softening" gospel truths or adding spurious practices to them.[65] We forget this at our peril, even as we celebrate the famous "catholic spirit" of George Whitefield, in this his 300th anniversary year.

---

[64] Fred Sanders, "Hit 'em with the Rock of Ages" at http://scriptoriumdaily.com/hit-em-with-the-rock-of-ages/ (November 11th, 2010).

[65] Whitefield was equally candid with Count Zinzendorff, often associated with Wesley and the Methodist movement, being astonished at the Moravian's use of images of Christ, incense, and other superstitious and idolatrous practices. See *The Works of the Reverend. George Whitefield*, vol.4: pp.253-261 (in a letter from April 1753).

St. Antholin's Lectureship Charity Lectures

In or about 1559 the parish of St. Antholin, now absorbed into what is the parish of St Mary-le-Bow in Cheapside and St Mary Aldermanbury, within the Cordwainer's Ward in the City of London, came into the possession of certain estates known as the 'Lecturer's Estates.' These were, it is believed, purchased with funds collected at or shortly after the date of the Reformation for the endowment of lectures, mid-week sermons or talks by Puritan preachers.

Over the centuries the funds were not always used for the stated purpose, and in the first part of the nineteenth century a scheme was drawn up which revivified the lectureship, which was to consist of forty lectures to be given three times a year on the "Puritan School of Divinity", the lecturer to receive one guinea per lecture. A further onerous requirement was that the lecturer had to be a beneficed Anglican, living within one mile of the Mansion House in the City of London.

Under such conditions the lectureship fell into disuse a long time ago, and it was not until 1987 that moves were put in hand with the Charity Commissioners to update the scheme. The first lecture under the new scheme was given in 1991.

Trustees: The Reverend W.T. Taylor
The Reverend Dr. M.E. Burkill
The Reverend Dr. L. Gatiss

St Antholin's Lectureship Charity Lectures

1991	J.I.Packer, *A Man for All Ministries: Richard Baxter 1651-1691.*
1992	Geoffrey Cox, *The Recovery and Renewal of the Local Church: the Puritan Vision.*
1993	Alister E. McGrath, *Evangelical Spirituality – Past Glories – Present Hopes – Future Possibilities.*
1994	Gavin J. McGrath, *'But We Preach Christ Crucified': The Cross of Christ in the Pastoral Theology of John Owen.*
1995	Peter Jensen, *Using the Shield of Faith – Puritan Attitudes to Combat with Satan.*
1996	J.I.Packer, *An Anglican to Remember – William Perkins: Puritan Popularizer.*
1997	Bruce Winter, *Pilgrim's Progress and Contemporary Evangelical Piety.*
1998	Peter Adam, *A Church 'Halfly Reformed' – the Puritan Dilemma.*
1999	J.I.Packer, *The Pilgrim's Principles: John Bunyan Revisited.*
2000	Ashley Null, *Conversion to Communion: Thomas Cranmer on a Favourite Puritan Theme.*
2001	Peter Adam, *Word and Spirit: The Puritan-Quaker Debate.*
2002	Wallace Benn, *Usher on Bishops: A Reforming Ecclesiology.*
2003	Peter Ackroyd, *Strangers to Correction: Christian Discipline and the English Reformation.*
2004	David Field, *'Decalogue' Dod and his Seventeenth Century Bestseller: A Four Hundredth Anniversary Appreciation.*
2005	Chad B. Van Dixhoorn, *A Puritan Theology of Preaching.*
2006	Peter Adam, *'To Bring Men to Heaven by Preaching' – John Donne's Evangelistic Sermons.*
2007	Tony Baker, *1807 – 2007: John Newton and the Twenty-first Century.*
2008	Lee Gatiss, *From Life's First Cry: John Owen on Infant Baptism and Infant Salvation.*
2009	Andrew Atherstone, *Evangelical Mission and Anglican Church Order: Charles Simeon Reconsidered*
2010	David Holloway, *Re-establishing the Christian Faith – and the Public Theology Deficit.*
2011	Andrew Cinnamond, *What matters in reforming the Church? Puritan Grievances under Elizabeth I.*
2012	Peter Adam, *Gospel Trials in 1662: To stay or to go?*
2013	Lee Gatiss, *Edmund Grindal – The Preacher's Archbishop*
2014	Lee Gatiss, *"Strangely Warmed" – Whitefield, Toplady, Simeon and Wesley's Arminian Campaigns*

St Antholin's Lectureship Charity Lectures

ed. Lee Gatiss, *Pilgrims, Warriors, and Servants: Puritan Wisdom for Today's Church: St Antholin lectures 1991-2000*

ed. Lee Gatiss, *Preachers, Pastors, and Ambassadors: Puritan Wisdom for Today's Church: St Antholin Lectures 2001-2010*